VOLUME 14

SING WITH THE CHOIR

CD INCLUDED

glee

Music From The FOX Television Sh

CW00348862

ISBN: 978-1-4234-9293-1

HAL•LEONARD®
CORPORATION

7777 W. BLUEMOUND RD. P.O. BOX 13819 MILWAUKEE, WI 53213

Visit Hal Leonard Online at
www.halleonard.com

CONTENTS

Can't Fight This Feeling

Original *GLEE* Arrangement by
ADAM ANDERS and **TIM DAVIS**
Adapted for publication by **ALAN BILLINGSLEY**

Words and Music by
KEVIN CRONIN

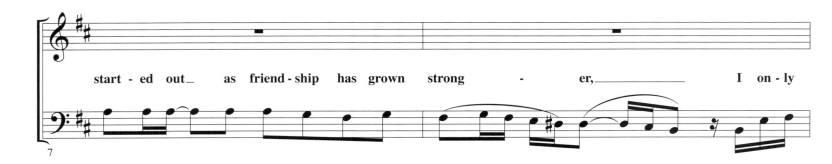

6

I've for-got-ten what I start-ed fight-in' for.

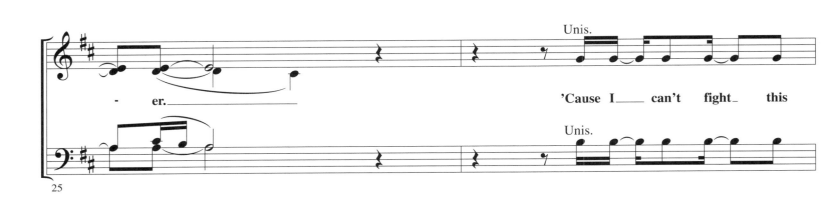

Unis. It's time to bring_ this ship in-to the shore_ and throw a-way the oars_ for-ev-

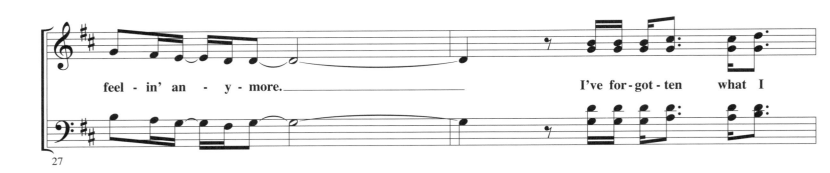

- er. Unis. 'Cause I___ can't fight_ this

feel-in' an-y-more._ I've for-got-ten what I

start-ed fight-in' for._ Unis. E-ven if I have_ to

crawl up - on your floor,_ come crash - ing through your door,_ ba - by,

I can't fight_ this feel - in' an - y - more._

I,_____ an - y - more._

My

Oo_

life has been_ such a whirl - wind since I saw___ you.___

I've been

Oo_

And it

run - nin' 'round in cir - cles in my mind._

al - ways seems that I'm_ fol - low - in' you,_____ boy,_____ 'cause you
(girl,)

take me to the plac - es that a - lone I'd nev - er find._____ And

42

e - ven as I wan - der, I'm keep - in' you__ in sight.__ You're a

Oo_____

45

can - dle in the win - dow__ on a cold, dark win - ter's night._____ And

can - dle in the win - dow__ on a cold, dark win - ter's night._ And

47

I'm get - ting clos - er than I._____ Ah_____

I'm get - ting clos - er than I___ ev - er thought_ I___ might._____

49

And I___ can't fight_ this feel - in' an - y - more._____

52

I've for-got-ten what I start-ed fight-in' for.

It's time to bring this ship in-to the shore and throw a-way the oars for-ev-

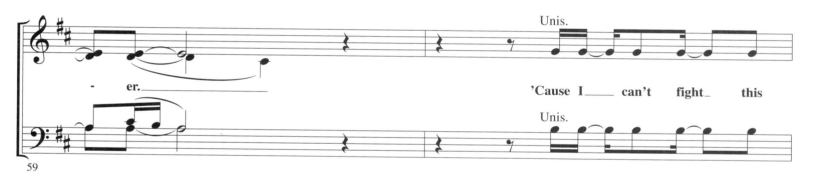

-er. 'Cause I can't fight this

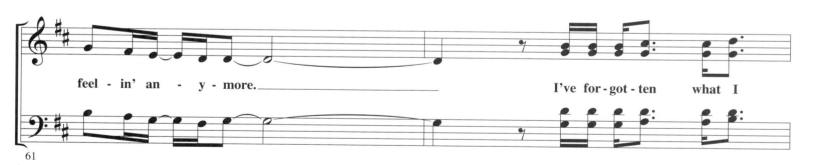

feel-in' an-y-more. I've for-got-ten what I

start-ed fight-in' for. E-ven if I have to

crawl up - on your floor,___ come crash - ing through your door,___ ba - by,

65

I can't fight___ this feel - in' an - y - more.___

I,_____ an - y - more.

67

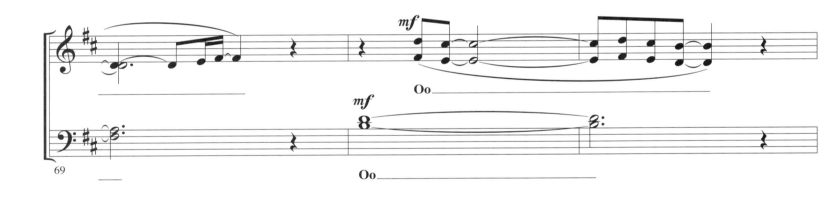

Oo___

Oo___

69

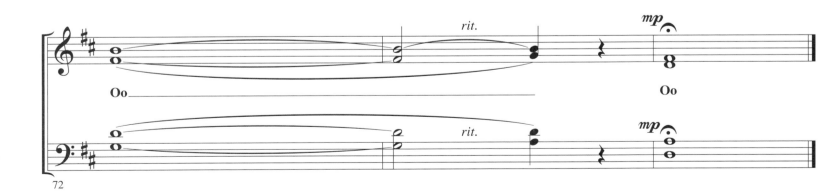

Oo___ Oo

72

Jump

**Original *GLEE* Arrangement by
ADAM ANDERS and TIM DAVIS
Adapted for publication by KIRBY SHAW**

**Words and Music by DAVID LEE ROTH,
EDWARD VAN HALEN, ALEX VAN HALEN
and MICHAEL ANTHONY**

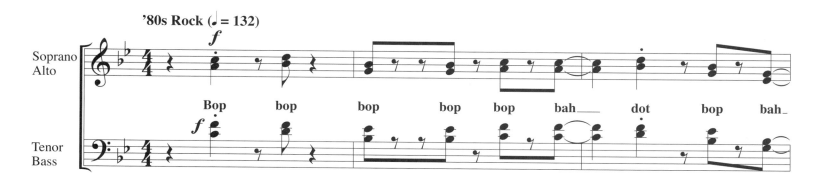

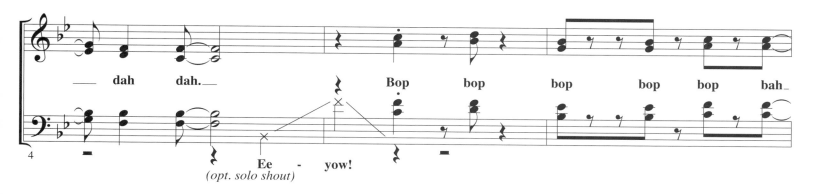

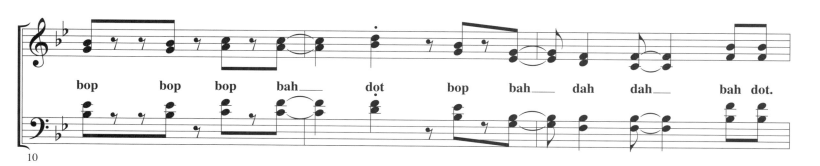

* "Migh's well" = Might as well

14

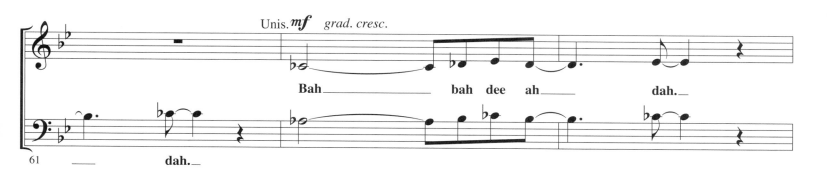

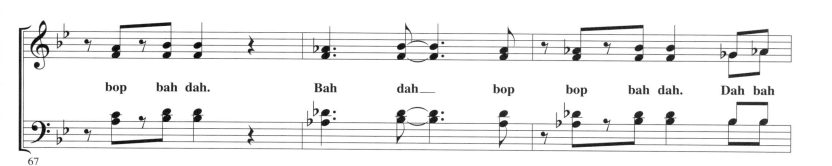

16

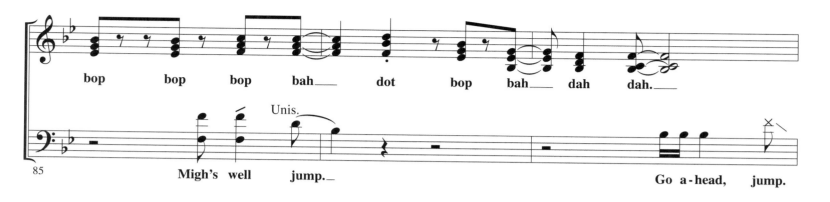

Don't Stop Believin'

**Original *GLEE* arrangement by
ADAM ANDERS and TIM DAVIS
Adapted for publication by ROGER EMERSON**

**Words and Music by STEVE PERRY,
NEAL SCHON and JONATHAN CAIN**

D.S. al Coda

nev - er ends;___ it goes on and on___ and on___ and on.___

D.S. al Coda

75

CODA

Dah dah dah dah (etc.)

Dah dah dah dah (etc.)

78

Dah dah dah dah___ (etc.)

81

Keep Holding On

Original *GLEE* arrangement by
ADAM ANDERS and TIM DAVIS
Adapted for publication by MAC HUFF

Words and Music by AVRIL LAVIGNE
and LUKASZ GOTTWALD

Ba ba ba ba ba   ba ba ba ba ba   ba ba ba ba ba   ba ba ba ba ba ba ba

1x - Female Solo
2x - Male Solo

You're not a - lone.____ To - geth - er we stand.____ I'll be by your
So far a - way,____ I wish you were here.____ Be - fore it's too

1x - Male Solo (top line)
2x - Duet

side, you know I'll take your hand. When it gets cold____ and it feels like the end,____
late, this could all dis - ap - pear. Be - fore the doors close____ and it comes to an end,____

there's no place to go,____ you know I won't give in.
with you by my side____ I will fight and de - fend.

Soprano

Alto
Ah ____

Tenor

Bass

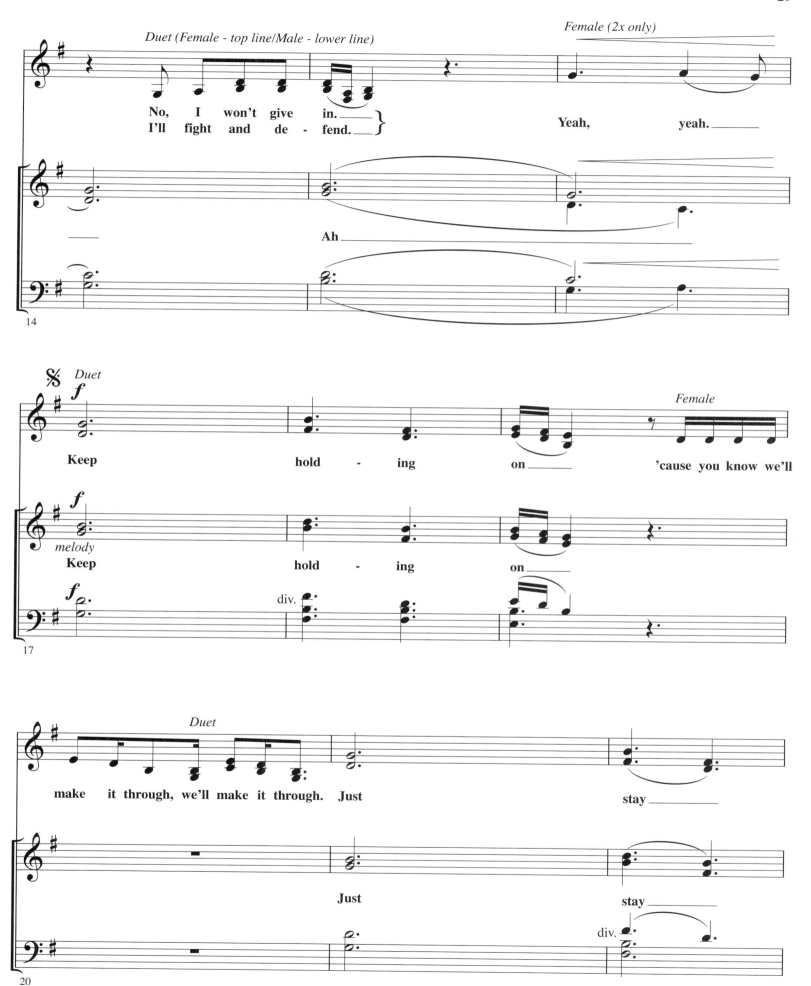

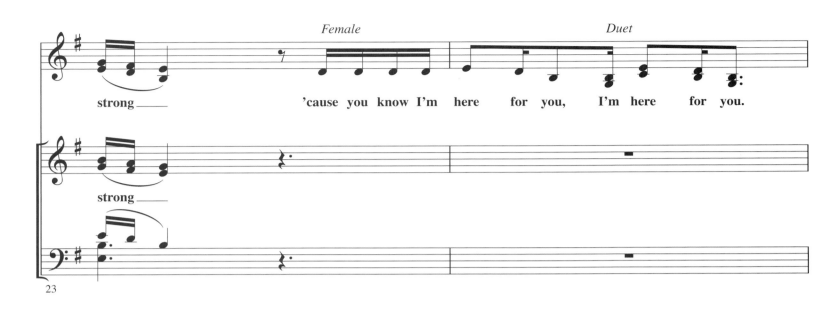

Female   *Duet*

strong _____ 'cause you know I'm here for you, I'm here for you.

strong _____

There's noth - ing you can say,   noth - ing you can do.

Unis.   div.   Unis.

noth - ing you can say,   noth - ing you can

Unis.   Unis.

There's no oth - er way when it comes __ to the truth _____ so keep

div.   *melody*

do,   when it comes __ to the truth _____ so keep

Unis.

32

Lean on Me

Original *GLEE* arrangement by
ADAM ANDERS and TIM DAVIS
Adapted for publication by ROGER EMERSON

Words and Music by
BILL WITHERS

38

42

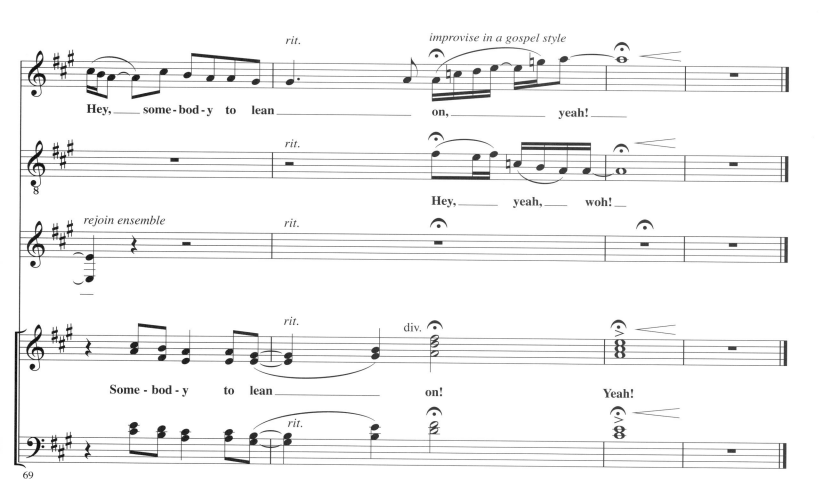

No Air

**Original *GLEE* arrangement by
ADAM ANDERS and TIM DAVIS
Adapted for publication by ALAN BILLINGSLEY**

**Words and Music by JAMES FAUNTLEROY II,
STEVEN RUSSELL, HARVEY MASON, JR.,
DAMON THOMAS and ERIK GRIGGS**

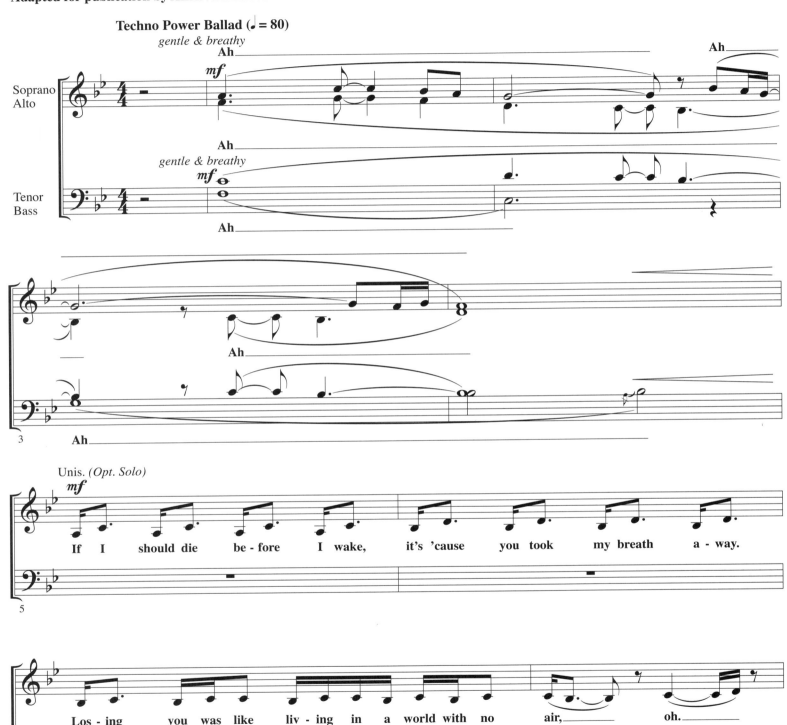

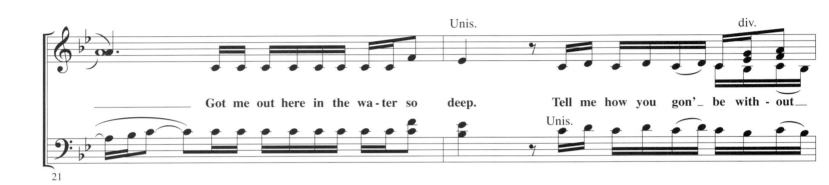

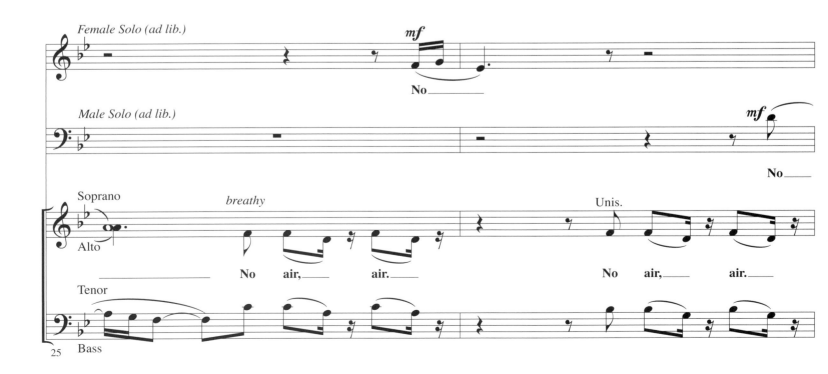

No - ho. _____

End Solo

End Solo

No air, _____ air. _____ No air, _____ air. _____

27

Soprano

Alto

I walked, I ran, I jumped, I flew right off the ground to float to you.

Tenor *mf*

29 Bass

There's no grav-i-ty to hold me down for real.

31

Some-how I'm still a-live in-side. You took my breath,_ but I_____ sur-vived.

33

48

50

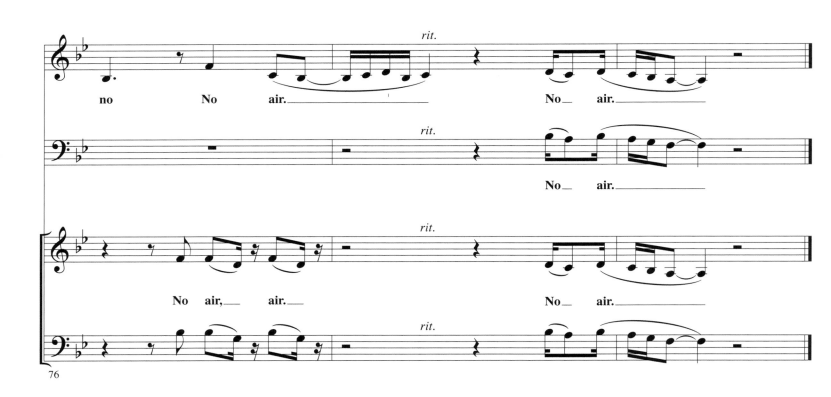

Rehab

Original *GLEE* Arrangement by
ADAM ANDERS and TIM DAVIS
Adapted for publication by MARK BRYMER

Words and Music by
AMY WINEHOUSE

They tried to make me go to re-

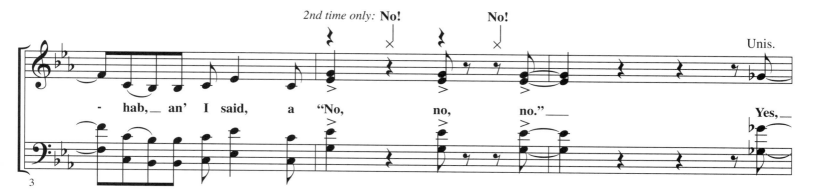

2nd time only: No! No!

-hab, an' I said, a "No, no, no." Yes,

I been black, but when I come back, you won't

2nd time only: No! No!

know, know, know.

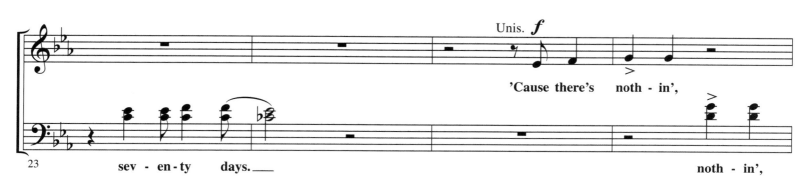

noth-ing you can teach me, Ah

that I can't learn

from Mis-ter Hath-a-way. (hay)

I did-n't get a lot in class, Whoa but I

know it don't come in a shot glass. They

D.S. al Coda

CODA

I won't ev-er wan-na drink a-gain. Ah

Somebody to Love

Original *GLEE* arrangement by
ADAM ANDERS and TIM DAVIS
Adapted for publication by ROGER EMERSON

Words and Music by
FREDDIE MERCURY

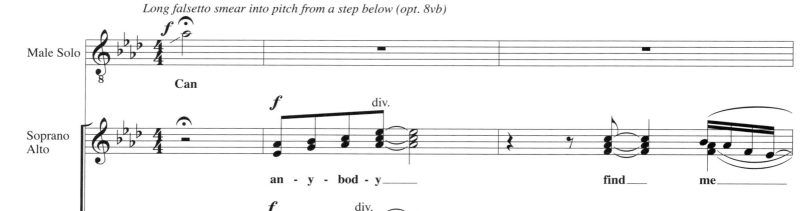

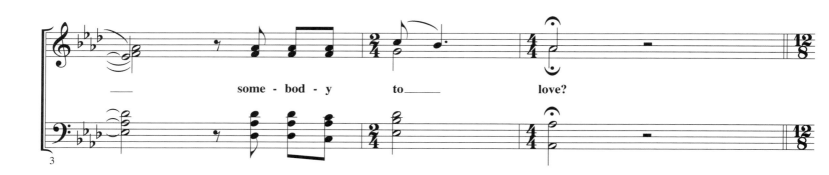

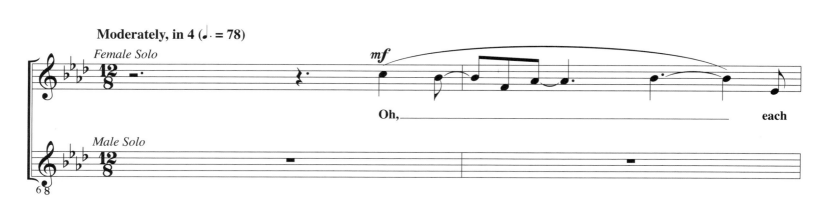

62

64

66

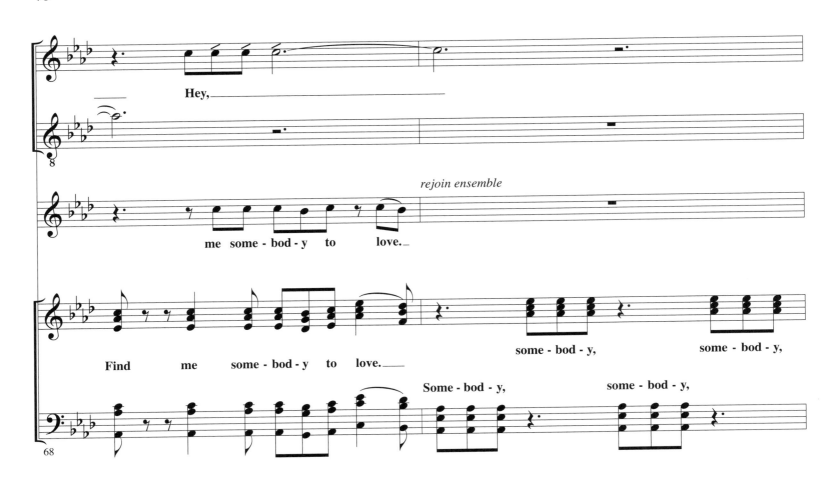